CW00687854

Tennis is mental too

Stephen Renwick

Acknowledgments

I would like to acknowledge the following people who have helped me with the making of the book and with my tennis playing and coaching career. A special thanks to James Bott who has produced another classic tennis book for me and to Andrea Fox for the illustrations. I would like to thank Clay Isles who did a fantastic job as a copywriter. Thanks to Alex Bogdanovic for giving permission to use his endorsement again. Thanks to God for giving me the gift of being able to play tennis. Thanks to Dr Andrew Peden for his great foreword. Thanks to Dr Wayne W. Dyer for giving me inspiration to keep going with the book and to complete it. Thanks to David Sammel and Jim Edgar for your input towards my book.

Personal thanks go to Rob Worthington, Nurshina Hirani, Syrah Hirani-Patel, Ilias Hirani-Worthington for all of their support and understanding of myself and my tennis. Thanks to Martin Fuller for all your help at the club. Thanks to everyone who has had coaching from me and for supporting my tennis coaching career.

Enjoy the book.

Big smiles

Stephen Renwick.

Contents

Tennis is mental, too.

The Author

Stephen Renwick has played tennis since he was 7. He played at county level and trained with one of the top junior squads in the country run by David Sammel and Jim Edgar. Stephen began coaching in 1994, taught in the U.S. and ran summer tennis clinics for Camp America. He has since coached tennis in Dubai, France and the UK. He has worked with some of the top coaches in the world and taught many high ranking players including Alex Bogdanovic, Chris Llewellyn and other leading British players. Stephen has dedicated his life to tennis and he is particularly interested in the psychology of the game. His first book, 'Tennis is Mental' became a best selling instructional sports book. The inspiration behind this work was a book by Tony Robbins, Unlimited Power. This describes how to take control of your life and achieve success. In 2005 Stephen appeared with the book on the BBC Two programme Dragons Den (2nd series), where he tried to raise £50,000 to help promote and distribute it worldwide. Stephen has learned a lot from the Dragons grilling.

Many top tennis players believe the psychology of the game is crucial in reaching one's potential. Stephen hopes you enjoy reading his book and that you learn some new mental skills that will enhance your tennis.

Foreword

This book is for any player, regardless of ability, who is serious about how the mental side of tennis can help them win. Backhands, serves or whatever, important as they are, can be improved with coaching and drills. But learning to utilise and manage a positive mental attitude brings another dimension to your game. Stephen Renwick draws upon his thousands of hours work with players at all levels, from beginners to British Davis Cup star Alex Bogdanovic. His knowledge of psychology and in particular neuro-linguistic programming (NLP) will help you analyse your performance so that you can identify which aspects of your game to replace or modify. This will inspire a new focused confidence, a mental toughness and self-belief that will separate you from the rest.

Remember that tennis is a sport played on a court and a game played in the mind. Good reading and better playing.

Andrew Peden PhD
Consultant Clinical Psychologist

Neuro Linguistic Programming

NLP is the study of human excellence
and how to influence and communicate
effectively with others. It was developed
in the 1970s by a team of psychologists
who were studying successful people in
order to analyse human behaviour. The
team included Richard Bandler
(psychologist), John Grinder (Linguist)
and Gregory Bateson (anthropologist).
They studied styles of language, patterns
in the brain and how words and actions
combine to make certain programmes
and patterns of behaviour.

NLP has now developed worldwide. It
offers insights into human behaviour and

improves performance. It is especially helpful in tennis. The unique process of NLP helps us interpret our experiences and to understand how we think, react and feel. It is recognised as a vital skill in human communication and has a major impact on how we regard and interpret the world around us. In tennis, NLP assists with goal setting, dealing with emotions, anxiety and stress. It also helps us develop positive thoughts and when to change beliefs and behaviour. Having worked with leading tennis players, I speak from experience about how the NLP helped them and how they progressed to new heights in terms of their results and rankings.

In Neuro Lingusitic Programming 'There are no unresourceful people, only unresourceful states.'

Neuro – relating to your brain and what happens in your mind.

Linguistic – relating to language and how you may use it effectively.

Programming – relating to patterns and programmes of behaviour which are learnt and repeated.

Neurological processes affect your thoughts, emotions and your physiology. These in turn affect your behaviour. Linguistic is the use of language to communicate with others and to influence your own experience of events. Programming is how you interpret situations and events and internal thoughts and patterns of behaviour. These help us evaluate situations, solve challenges and make decisions.

NLP can be used in sport, business and personal development. The skills are beneficial for professional athletes, organisations, teams, sport coaches and parents. I have personally used NLP in my own life and within companies and also with professional athletes. In tennis terms NLP is based on the following concepts.

1: Players respond to their own experience, not to reality itself.

2: Players with choices are better than players without one.

3: Players make the best choice they have at the time.

4: Players actions have a positive intent.

5: Players unconscious minds balance their conscious.

6: Players have all the resources they need or they can create them.

7: Mind and body are one system.

8: Players process through their senses.

9: Modelling on successful players leads to excellence.

I have tried to use as little NLP jargon as possible. In this way you should begin to get a feel for NLP. If you are familiar with NLP and its techniques you will find this book easy to understand. NLP is most commonly known through the work of such people as Tony Robbins and Paul Mckenna.

Introduction

Why the mental side of tennis is so important

Have you ever lost a tennis match you were certain you should have won? In a tough match do you sometimes give up? Is concentration difficult? Does your mind wander? 'Choking', playing 'tight', getting 'the elbow' all express the nervousness that every player feels from time to time. Perhaps you are particularly prone. Can you keep calm during a match or do you give way to anger, frustration or perhaps even racket throwing? How do you react when your opponent or the umpire makes a line call you feel is unjust?

All players experience these kinds of

problems. You can't play the game in a mental vacuum. The mind is as much a part of the game as hitting forehands or backhands. How you cope with the mental stresses provides much of the challenge and fun.

Being 'inside the zone' is current jargon for playing at the top of your game. Everything flows, errors are few and your tennis seems effortless. Other times the reverse happens. Movement is lethargic or heavy, you can't keep focused and errors abound. Sometimes these two opposite states shift from one to the other during the course of the same match.

A tennis player's game is divided into 4 areas: technical, tactical, physical and mental. Take a lesson with a coach and the chances are they will spend most of their time, if not all, on the technical. They will explain the deficiencies of your serve, backhand or whatever and how to put them right. Passing reference may be paid to footwork or some tactical ploy. The mental processes, however, the inner powers you bring, the concentration and disciplines necessary to engage the other three will scarcely get a look in. This book redresses that balance.

"Why does tennis cause this mental upheaval in so many players?"

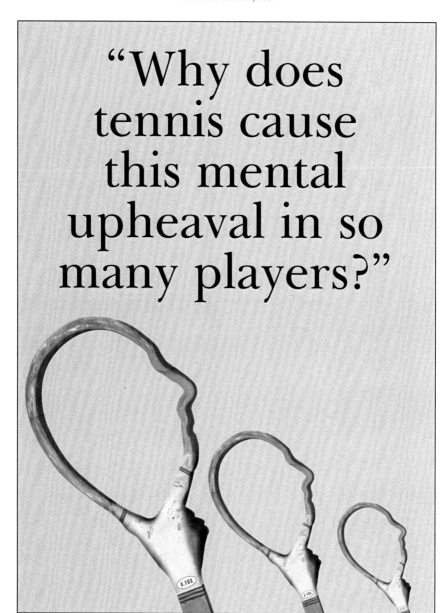

CHAPTER 1

Tennis Mentality

When 2 players take the court for a match their attitudes can be said to resemble the sides of a pair of scales. Both optimistic about their chances of winning, they are equally balanced. Within a few games, if one player has taken the lead, the balance has shifted. You can tell that from the player's body language. The losing player's shoulders have sunk, they may look dejected or have become more volatile. Away from tennis the person may be well-balanced and rational. Yet on a tennis court he or she doesn't seem to be able to cope. Why does tennis cause this mental upheaval in so many players?

Among other things tennis requires a combination of timing, decision-making, co-ordination, focus, speed and physical fitness. In an average tennis match, a player makes about 1000 decisions, most of them made in under a second. Which shot? Where to hit it? What spin? How high? How hard? Time and time again. Top players respond automatically. Thousands of hours on the practice court have given them the ability to hit the ball instinctively so that decision making is more an instant reaction than a moment of judgement. Roger Federer would otherwise never be able to pull off his superlative reflex shot making, sometimes played under the most extreme pressure.

Technique also needs to be finely tuned. The speed and power of modern tennis give little scope for ragged and insecure methods of hitting the ball.

A tennis match is full of 'dead time'; moments, minutes between points, changing ends when the ball is not in play. In a typical tennis match less than a quarter of the match is spent playing. The rest is the interval between points. These spaces lay like traps for the unwary. Matches are lost because of them as the mind loses its focus and starts to wander. No wonder that tennis is very much a mental battle. There is so much time to think. The player who keeps their attention, their determination, their plan of action, while alert to the possibility they may have to change it, will achieve the upper hand.

Factors that determine the ideal mental state include:

Line calling: Only top tournaments provide umpires. Most tennis matches are played without one and players call their own lines. Doubtful calls can lead to tempers rising and aggressive behaviour. All this stress adds to the mental pressure.

No half time: Matches are continuous. You are not allowed to take breaks or bring on a substitute.

On show: During a match there is nowhere to hide. You are on your own. People can see how you are playing, your mistakes, how you behave and react to competition.

No one can help you: You are not allowed to receive coaching (apart from in the Davis

Cup). You have to work things out for yourself.

Time limits: You never run out of time during a tennis match as you do in many other games which are of fixed duration. This keeps the final outcome uncertain and means that no matter how far behind you are there is still time to fight back.

Competition: Many players, especially at a lower level, shy away from competition. When they do enter a tournament or an event, nerves often get the better of them. They lack proper match experience.

Match play: Sometimes people develop a knack for winning but don't look as if they should beat anybody. They may have unorthodox or odd technique. They have discovered that not making errors counts for more than trying to hit winners. These are often the most difficult players to beat. They thrive on competition and love the challenge. They have all the determination of a top class player but lack the talent. As an opponent they are every club player's nightmare.

Fun: Everybody enjoys winning. Nobody likes losing. The fun comes from the challenge of trying to win and drives the acquisition of technical, physical, tactical and mental skills.

Do you practise mental skills?

Do you find that puzzling? You practise forehands and backhands, why not then the mental side of the game? Players spend hours in their clubs doing drills, hitting balls, taking lessons. Some play matches. Rarely do they attend to their mental state. When they play a match they often attribute winning or losing to how well or badly they concentrated or if they were nervous. Concentration or controlling nerves therefore does feature in what they feel they ought to be aware of. Why then don't they practise them?

Most matches are decided by points played at critical stages. In a close encounter the player with the least number of won points can even end up the winner. They have simply won the important points. Most matches are won on ability so when you play someone of a similar standard you should have an equal chance of winning or losing. You might play a match on Sunday and win 6-2 6-0, yet a week later lose to the same opponent. Why? Your fitness can't have altered. More probable is that your mental attitude has changed and hence a different outcome.

You may have been over confident going into the second match. You may therefore have played casually and allowed your opponent to take the upper hand early on. So, from a position of over confidence you were suddenly playing with a lack of it and lost. This simple example happens time and time again at all levels of play. It shows how vital it is to be alert to one's own mental state. It is therefore surprising that so little time is spent improving it.

"When we are angry we expend more emotional energy and our thinking is likely to be disrupted."

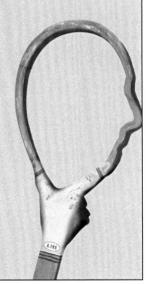

CHAPTER 2

Mental 'States'

A mental 'state' is how we are at any given moment. It combines our physiology, thinking and emotions. We experience these states within ourselves but they show external signs - pulse rate, blood pressure - that can be measured. These measures do not tell us how it feels to be angry because of a missed shot or how we feel when we win. The state we are in affects our experience on the court. The calmer we are, for example, the easier it is to think rationally. When we are angry we expend more emotional energy and our thinking is likely to be disrupted. I have seen players so angry they have almost lost control. In this state they have little chance of beating anyone. Anxiety also makes it harder to co-ordinate our muscles.

Our states always have emotional components. The good news is that they change during the peaks and troughs of a tennis match. Negative sensations therefore, do not last forever. The emotional state we are in affects our capabilities. An example of this is the difference between playing with no one watching and when there are spectators. Our emotions change when people watch.

When you play you should be aware of how you are mentally so that you can try to access your (IPS) Ideal Performance State. Often called 'in the zone', it is when you are unaware of time; you feel you are floating, the ball seems bigger. When Ivan

Lendl won the 1986 US Open he recalled how confident he felt. 'No matter how hard I hit the ball, it always went in.' During that tournament he was able to summon an ideal mentality in every match. He was allowing things to happen rather than trying to make them happen.

Playing in the zone happens to many players, no matter their standard. For most of them it happens only occasionally. The ideal is to invoke it at will.

Tennis players often try to galvanise themselves into a peak state. They pump their fists, skip around the court and talk to themselves - 'Come on', 'Let's go.' Their language and physiology allow them rapidly to change states.

The way you use your body affects your mind and ultimately your performance on court. Your body language doesn't only show how you are. It can also dictate how you want to be. Sit on a comfortable chair and give a wide, beaming smile. Breathe deeply and sit up tall and strong. Now, try to feel depressed. It's impossible. Being mentally tough means having the ability to control your mental states on the court regardless of events. Top players remain mentally strong by:

Having an unshakeable belief in their ability.

Being like a rubber ball that readily bounces back from adversity.

Having faith that their skills and capabilities are better than those of their opponent.

Sustaining the ability to stay focused on the task when faced with challenges during competition.

Having a positive motivational style.

Dealing effectively with unexpected events and coping with those beyond their control.

If you can become aware of your own mental states and adjust them according to the above principles you will notice a great improvement in your match play. You will become mentally tougher.

A major distinction between all states is being associated or disassociated. If you are associated it means you are reliving the experience as though it is happening through your own eyes. Disassociation means being outside the experience.

Association is being inside an experience - with it, in the heat of it, going with the flow, in touch, in the zone.

Disassociation is where you feel things

from outside - not with it, out of touch, not quite there, time passing by, laid back, had enough, spaced out.

Try it out for yourself.

Think of a time when you lost a match you should have won. Run the experience through your mind like a movie clip. See yourself losing match point, walking to the net to shake hands. Don't view this from the outside but make sure you are in the picture, looking through your own eyes. See what you saw, hear what you heard, smell what you smelt. How do you feel? Are there any intense emotional feelings? This way of seeing events is known as associated.

Now try disassociation. Run the same movie clip in your mind, but this time watch yourself from a distance. See yourself in the picture, but keep yourself outside. How do you feel? You should feel less intense than being associated.

Association and Disassociation are more than just ways of looking at mental pictures. They are ways of changing the way you feel about experiences. Some times you may feel totally with it. Other times you may feel out there, in the clouds.

Association is a good way to relive an enjoyable experience - maybe a great match you played or an amazing shot you hit. It is also ideal for practising techniques and performing skills.

Disassociation is best for reviewing painful experiences, learning from mistakes and getting over negative memories.

Here is an NLP exercise to experience association and disassociation.

1: Think of a pleasant memory of a tennis match you recently played.

2: What sort of picture do you have in your mind?

3: Are you looking through your own eyes (associated)?

4: Are you disassociated, watching yourself playing tennis?

5: Whichever way it is, change the way you view it.

6: Now go back to how you were before.

7: Which method do you prefer?

For most players being associated recalls more intense feelings than being disassociated. In a disassociated state you probably feel more out of touch than if you are fully associated. Reviewing your best matches in this manner is a great way to bring back good feelings so that you can access them as you want. This is particularly useful if you have played an awful match and want to neutralise your negative emotions.

The mind cannot tell the difference between a real image and a made-up one. "

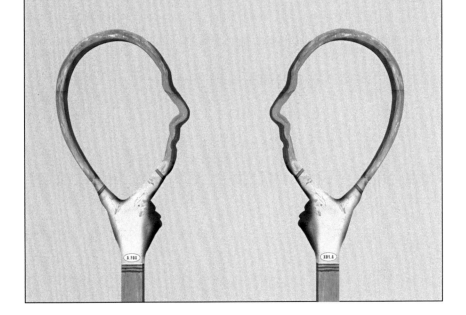

CHAPTER 3

Mental Imagery

Mental imagery is often described as visualisation or mental rehearsal. You create or recreate situations in your mind. In NLP they are known as submodalities. They look at the pictures in your mind, the sounds associated with them and how they make you feel. This could be imagining yourself serving with good technique, following through on your forehand or hitting a great passing shot.

The mind cannot tell the difference between a real image and a made-up one. Mental imagery can therefore be a very powerful tool in improving your game.

- Visual submodalities use colour, brightness, distance, clarity, focus, location, movement, perspective and orientation.

- Auditory submodalities include volume, location, direction, duration, tone/pitch, tempo, timbre, mono or stereo.

- Kinaesthetic submodalities suggest location, intensity, temperature, texture, pressure, movement, speed, direction, duration and humidity.

These different submodalities can help you change the way you feel and how you behave. Think of a tennis match when you played well and see what comes to mind. What is the image? Is it in colour? Is it close? Are there any sounds? Are you in the picture or looking at yourself from outside? Now, compare this to a time when you played badly. What do you see? Is the image black and white? Is it a dull picture? How do you look? What is your body posture?

There should be fundamental differences between the two. When you want to practice imagery, make sure your images are colourful, bright, close up and with sounds that motivate you.

Imagery creates a physiological response. Imagined events produce an innervation in your muscles similar to when you were doing the act in real life. You are using similar neural pathways. Imagining yourself performing strengthens those neural pathways that control certain muscle groups.

Imagery also helps you understand the patterns of movement required to perform certain skills and techniques. It provides a mental blueprint that your brain can then use to send out the signals to the muscles.

Mental imagery can also be a confidence booster. It can lower anxiety, improve concentration and act as a spur to motivation. You can imagine beating players you have lost to in the past simply by running through a match against them. Next time you play them you will feel much more confident.

Try the following exercises.

Sit down, close your eyes and picture a room you know well other than the one you are in. Place yourself so that you can see the entire room. Have a look around and take note of all the details. What can you see? What textures and shapes are there? Is the room warm or cold? Can you feel the air on your skin? Use all of your senses.

Now think of one of your best matches, where everything went really well and you played outstanding tennis. Run that movie in your mind. Look at things through your own eyes and relive the experience. How does it feel? Is the picture in full colour? Are there spectators? If there are, do they clap? What are you saying to yourself? See how you feel hitting the ball in the sweet spot. What can you taste or smell? Play around with the imagery. The more colourful and attractive the image the more powerful it will be and the more exciting it will be for you.

When you are preparing for a match try the following:

Imagine yourself walking onto the court to practise, feeling light and athletic. Your shots have great shape, feel good and are powerful and easy. There is a flowing compact swing and a great follow through. You are floating around court with no effort and you can hit the opponent's shots back with precision.

Now you go to the net and warm up your volleys and smashes, hitting the ball deep and in front, feeling good under the ball. You hit a crisp forehand volley and then put away an overhead with ease. Your legs are feeling strong and full of energy.

As you move back to warm up your serve you feel the motion is smooth and the ball toss is in the right place, transferring your body weight forward and in the direction of the ball. You hit the ball exactly where you aimed and you feel in control and confident.

Imagine the start of the match and see yourself serving well and taking the initiative. Visualise hitting powerful first serves which your opponent scrapes back mid court and you easily step in and put the ball away into the corners.

The next point, you serve and begin a baseline rally where you are moving freely, smoothly and striking the ball with ease and power. You see yourself hitting the lines and moving your opponent outside the tramlines. Finally, your opponent hits a weak crosscourt angle and you slice down the line and approach the net. Then he attempts a lob, but you are on top of the net and simply bury the ball into the court and over the netting at the back.

On the first point of the next game you hit a backhand passing shot and get off to a good start breaking your opponent's serve. You feel totally confident and focused. It's only a matter of time before you are shaking hands at the net with another win under your belt.

It is a good idea to use imagery after practising because you are already familiar with the shots and you can feel them more easily. Try it for 5 to 10 minutes after a practice. Do this regularly and it will really compliment your on court practice. Another good time is before competition, especially if you have a big match coming up. This prepares you for moments of pressure so that you can deal with various challenges in the match. Mental imagery is also beneficial when you are injured and helps you keep in touch with skills and techniques with which you are already familiar.

Imagery Questionnaire

Because imagery can involve visual, auditory, olfactory, gustatory and kinaesthetic senses, it is important to break it down. You may also experience certain moods and emotions connected to your imagery.

Over the page are three situations in tennis. Imagine each scenario as vividly as you can and try to make the picture as real to life as possible. Then rate your imagery on the following NLP dimensions:

Visual:

1 = No image to

5 = Extremely vivid images.

Auditory:

1 = No sounds to

5 = Extremely clear sounds

Kinaesthetic:

1 = No sensations to

5 = Extremely clear sensations of making the movement.

Emotions:

1 = No feelings to

5 = Extremely clear feelings

As you try to remember each moment think back to a time when the event happened. Remember the day and the weather. Was it hot or cold? Was it windy? Was the sun shining? Were birds singing?

Were other people there? Were there other matches or people on different courts? What were you wearing? What was your opponent wearing?

1. Your best ever performance

Close your eyes and imagine the match as clearly as possible. Re-live it, seeing what you saw, hearing what you heard and feeling the way you felt. Think of a specific time when you played unstoppable tennis and you were in the zone.

How clear was your image? Use the scales as mentioned above 1-5

A. Visual

C. Kinaesthetic

B. Auditory

D. Emotions

2. Practice with your coach

Do the same exercise as 1 but this time with your tennis coach. See yourself make a mistake. Imagine the situation again. Run this like a movie in your mind and answer the same four sense questions.

How clear was your image? Use the scales as mentioned above 1-5

A. Visual

C. Kinaesthetic

B. Auditory

D. Emotions

3. When you felt totally confident

Think back to that moment. Nothing went wrong, you had all day to hit the ball and you knew you could make any shot. Run this experience in your mind and answer the following again.

A. Visual

C. Kinaesthetic

B. Auditory

D. Emotions

Scores

Now you need to total up your imagery scores and determine what they mean. Add up the ratings for your answers and record the results on the following table:

Visual_____ + _____ + _____ =

Auditory_____ + _____ + _____ =

Kinaesthetic_____ + _____ + _____ =

Emotions_____ + _____ + _____ =

The maximum total for any section is 15 and the minimum is 3. The nearer to 15 in any of the senses the better skills you show for that dimension of imagery. Where the score is lower, you need to work on developing that sense to improve your imagery power.

You should find images more powerful in an associated state - reliving events through your own eyes - as opposed to the disassociated one, watching yourself perform.

Chunking makes it easier to achieve a long-term goal by breaking down the desired end result.

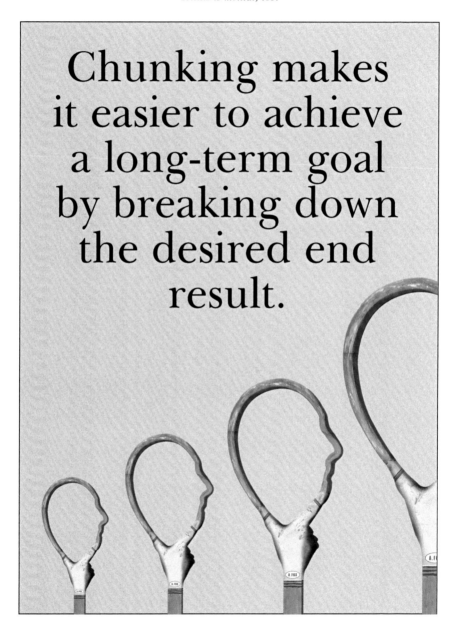

CHAPTER 4

Goal Setting

Tennis players need to set themselves clear goals and outcomes.

Decide what is most important to you so that you can prioritise your goals. Setting priorities helps you remain focused and steers your day-to-day behaviour. Goals can be broken down into process, performance and outcome. Here are possible areas in your game on which you could focus:

Rating Scale

1 = Very Important
2 = Important
3 = Not Very Important

Skill to improve

Importance Score 1, 2 or 3

Footwork

First Serve %

2nd serve

Consistency

Volleys

Smash

Mid court play

Backhand slice

Backhand crosscourt

Forehand crosscourt

Mental toughness

Concentration

Pre-match preparation

Post-match routine

Prioritise the areas you want to improve to determine what is most important to you. Now set goals around your strengths and weaknesses.

When you have established your goals you can plan how to improve that area. Bear in mind the benefits of 'chunking'. Chunking makes it easier to achieve a long-term goal by breaking down the desired end result. Imagine trying to eat a whole birthday cake in one go. It would prove too much. Separating the cake into small digestible chunks would make it easier. Effective goal setting is about meeting objectives that lead you onto bigger objectives.

Have a look at your priorities. Set some

short and long term goals based on the areas you want to improve.

Here is an example:

Priority goal:

1: Improve 1st serve percentage from 50% to 70%

Short term goal: Make at least 3 first serves a game by taking pace off the ball and using more height over the net.

Process: Practice 1st serves each session, working on consistency. Make the practice as similar to a match as possible.

Performance: Have a coach or a friend keep a tally of how many 1st serves you make in your next few matches.

Outcome: Have you raised your 1st serve percentage? What results have you produced?

Long term goal: To be able to hit 70% of first serves in with different pace, placement and spin under pressure in a match.

Process:

Performance:

Outcome:

Another method of goal setting is an NLP technique called 'well formed outcomes'. This breaks down goals and gives a clear sense of why you want to do something. I used this strategy with Alex Bogdanovic and we both saw how successful it was. Players using these techniques clearly understand why they are doing something. This insight gives them power and the ability to really focus on their goals. Having used the traditional SMART goals setting process, I found the NLP outcomes to be more effective.

NLP Well Formed Outcomes

What do you want?

Well Formed Outcomes are targets, goals or objectives that have been systematically designed by ensuring they fit the criteria below. The benefit of this process is that goals become more achievable and realistic, hence the name 'well formed'. The process of going through the six questions creates a detailed internal representation in your mind of exactly what you want to achieve, enhancing your belief. The outcome process helps you focus on what you want, not what you don't want. This keeps your attention on what to do and how to do it, rather than looking at problems, excuses and explanations. This process also helps rapport. It is a great way to get to know somebody very quickly on a personal or professional level. It highlights any areas where you may need to adapt or change a specific behaviour. The outcome steps act as a framework that keeps discussions and activities on track. This can be in business, sport, counselling or personal coaching.

1. Positive wants

   What exactly do you want as a player?

   Evidence of tennis success

   Evidence of success

2. How will you recognise this (Results & Rankings)

   How will others know when you have this?

3. Context (When & Where)

   When and where do you want to achieve this goal?

   What you can achieve

   The outcome needs to be within your control.

4. What resources do you need in order to achieve this?

   What do you need to do to achieve this?

   Is this something you can achieve yourself or does it require other people?

5. Advantages & Disadvantages

   There are always disadvantages when making a change.

   What will achieving cost you?

   What are the disadvantages of making this change?

   What are the advantages of making this change?

   Worthwhile

   Motivation

6. What is important to you about getting this?

   What will be the benefit of this outcome?

   What will achieving these outcomes enable you to avoid?

I have used these NLP aids with several top world ranked tennis players and the results have been amazing. To use these effectively, decide what it is that you want and then answer the rest of the questions. This process is more powerful than traditional goal setting as you gain more sensory specific reasons for doing something. Try it and see for yourself.

Motivation.

Motivation rcinforces all the advice in this book. It is the guiding factor that endorses all the other skills.

The psychology of motivation stems from why we do things.

Motives

These are hypothetical states producing behaviour that take us towards our goals.

They cannot be seen or measured but they are shown in our behaviour. Our motives can take the form of needs, drives and incentives, which are also inferred, from behaviour. Survival depends on us meeting our physiological needs - food, oxygen, drink, avoiding pain, eliminating waste and being in the right temperature environment. Psychologically we need achievement, self-esteem, approval (social) and power. Our needs therefore give rise to our drives. Hunger, for example, raises the drive for food. The longer we go without something the more intense the drive. In today's modern tennis world, the drive for achievement is high and this motivates most top players. Roger Federer has a strong achievement motivational drive. He wants to win more grand slams and be remembered as one of the greatest players ever.

When you are motivated you achieve more. It is therefore important to discover what motivates you.

Sports psychologists refer to intrinsic and extrinsic motivation. Intrinsic means being motivated from the inside, extrinsic by external events. Intrinsic motivation is having feelings of satisfaction and fulfilment. Extrinsic is having rewards or punishment (or both) from outside.

Most successful tennis players are intrinsically motivated because they aim at self-mastery and increasing their ability to deal with the environment that tennis creates. As players develop and become more successful the amount of money they receive from winnings and endorsements makes them more extrinsically motivated. Motivation is also closely linked to the goals you have because these can drive you to achieve and help you reach your target. Performance goals are better than outcome goals because they help you improve by developing your game rather than just focusing on winning a match. This approach also enables you to practice specific areas so that you can improve for the next match.

You cannot always control the outcome of a match because uncontrollable events - bad line calls, injuries and mishits etc – might work against you. How your opponent plays also obviously determines the outcome of the match. It therefore makes more sense to focus on playing each point to the best of your ability. The outcome then takes care of itself.

NLP uses terms towards being motivated

and away from being motivated. These describe how people are driven by their motivation. Some people I have worked with have been strongly inclined towards being motivated. This could be wanting to be ranked in the top 10 juniors in the country or break into the world top 100. Their motive is driving them to reach their target and pulling them towards it and this gives them pleasure. Other players behave away from being motivated. This means they want to move away from pain. These players need painful experiences to keep driving them forwards. Losing to someone becomes the driving force to improve so that they won't repeat the loss. The disadvantage of this type of motivation is that you always need to experience pain to get anywhere. With towards motivation you are going forwards and experiencing more pleasurable experiences.

Visualisation and watching your favourite players is another useful form of motivation and can help you reach your ideal match arousal levels. This is also linked into modelling (NLP) where you play as if you were somebody else. I remember watching Michael Chang playing at the French Open and then trying to play as if I was Chang. I began to copy (unconsciously at the time) certain behaviours of Chang and the way he played the game. I had a two handed backhand then, was about the same height as Chang and played from the baseline. This really motivated me on an intrinsic level and I stayed on court for hours hitting balls. Every player should study how top professionals hit the ball. This can be very motivating, especially when the player hits a great winner, inspiring you to try to make the same shot yourself.

"Confident players usually set challenging goals for themselves and actively pursue them."

CHAPTER 5

Confidence

'Whether you say you can or you say you can't, you are right'

Henry Ford

Although confidence springs from competence, working hard on court during practice is also crucial. Hard work enhances self-belief and increases confidence in your ability. I also know through working in NLP with players that confidence is a state we can enter when we need to. If you have been confident before, you can access that state again. Confidence also gives you the ability to figure out a winning strategy when you're playing.

Some players lack confidence and doubt their own ability. They are pessimistic about their chances of winning and often expect to lose. Having confidence that you can win a match is vital. Without it you are defeated before you start.

Confidence increases effort and the amount of work a player puts in relates to their self-confidence. Most matches are against similar standard players. The player who puts in the most effort usually wins.

Confidence also affects your goals because confident players usually set challenging goals for themselves and actively pursue them. Players maximise their performance and their commitment by setting these goals. This increases their confidence. It's a cycle of success.

Confidence allows players to be more task-focused. They are less distracted by outside events. Lack of confidence causes anger over a missed shot or worry about what people might think. Being confident also helps you to remain calm under pressure, enabling you to play more positively. In the final set the more confident player has the best chance of winning.

Sometimes people try not to lose a match rather than playing to win it. These attitudes to match play produce completely different strategies on court. Matches often come down to shot selection at critical points. Confidence allows you to hit your shots properly. Players who lack confidence often push the ball or steer it, hoping their opponent misses. They either play too safely or take unnecessary risks. This means they panic, often over hit and attempt glory shots at times of pressure. There should be a balance between going for your shots and allowing a margin for error, especially on important points.

Tennis matches ebb and flow. There is sometimes a momentum when a player wins several games in a row then loses a similar number in succession. They may win one set and lose the next 6-0. There are times when it's all going well and then a bad line call changes the rhythm of the match. The shift can be linked to confidence and self-belief.

The difference between a player who comes back and a player who crumbles is often confidence. Players like Andre Agassi and Lleyton Hewitt who fight until the last ball are very confident in their ability. Agassi also worked hard on his physical conditioning, helping him feel more and more confident, especially in 5 set matches.

A player's lack of confidence usually means a low-level performance leading to losing the match. Lack of confidence causes worrying, giving up, focusing on errors, anxiety and playing tentatively.

Confidence can change very quickly. A player warms up well, serves fantastically and then starts the match by pushing the ball defensively. Other times players perform well for two sets, suddenly miss an easy shot and throw it all away. This often happens on big points and at crucial stages in the match.

Overconfidence is another hazard. Some players believe their abilities are greater than they are and underestimate their opponent. It gives them a false sense of confidence. This occurs when two unevenly matched players compete against each other. This is why top ranked players can lose to players nobody has heard of. Tim Henman, for example, has sometimes beaten a player in the top 5 only to lose in the next round to somebody outside the first 200.

Accessing your confidence using NLP:

Hold your head up high and sit or stand comfortably with your shoulders relaxed. Support yourself by your spine and imagine a piece of string lifting you from the scalp up into the sky. Stay relaxed, feel supported by this string. This is the neutral position of your confidence state.

Now, think of a time when you were totally confident. Enter that scene as if it was happening right now. Go inside, see what you saw, and hear what you heard. How good do you feel? If you can't think of a time imagine how you would look if you felt confident. Imagine yourself with all the power, shots and ability you could ever need. Make the images bigger, brighter and richer. Increase the sounds in the scene until they are clearer and more exciting. Immerse yourself in an overall feeling of confidence.

Feel in which part of your body confidence is the strongest and give this feeling a colour. Move the colour of confidence to the top of your head and all the way down to your feet. Fill your entire body with this colour and feel the sensations of confidence.

Repeat this process 3-4 times.

We mentioned earlier about the mind

and body being one system and how our thoughts, feelings, emotions and behaviours are interrelated and can affect one another. This means it is important to act confidently. The more you behave in this way the more likely you will feel confident. This is crucial, particularly when a match is not going your way. Your confidence levels may be low, whilst your opponent's confidence is growing. It is important to display a confident, positive image when things are against you. You need to force your personality into the mind of the opponent making them see you as calm, confident and assured of success even though the score is against you. Try never to let the opponent know when you doubt yourself. Players will then think losing doesn't bother you. There are many non-verbal signals you can give off such as walking with head held high, breathing fully, skipping and clenching your fist, all of which demonstrate positive body language. The alternative is to become angry, stressed, unhappy and complaining. This shows the opponent how weak you are and in turn boosts their confidence.

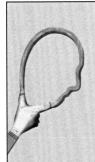

"A game plan provides a structure and direction for your match."

CHAPTER 6

Mental Preparation

It's surprising how many players pay little attention to preparing for their matches. It often makes the difference between winning and losing and is a vital part of being a successful match player. All it needs is a plan of action with various strategies. A game plan provides a structure and direction for your match. Not planning ahead is like driving into an unknown city without a map. Without a clear game plan everything becomes haphazard and you find it hard deciding how to play your opponent. A pre-match plan gives you a mental map of how you are going to play and helps to keep you focused.

First make a list of your opponent's strengths and weaknesses. Then match them against your own skills. It's a big help if you have played your opponent before. If you haven't, try to watch them in action, answering the following questions:

Which player won most baseline points?

Was the opponent a good volleyer?

How effective were your opponent's 1st and 2nd serves?

What was your opponent's smashing like?

Was your opponent a serve and volleyer? If so, how often and was it always on first serve?

What was your opponent's return of serve like?

Did your opponent have a favourite passing shot? Down the line or cross-court?

Did the opponent keep fighting or did they crack under pressure?

How did your opponent play critical points?

How did your opponent move? Were they fast or slow about the court?

Did they hit drop shots?

Now you have assessed your opponent do the same with your own game. Match up your strengths against your opponent's weaknesses. Remember, it is how your shots perform under pressure that counts. A successful strategy cannot be based on inconsistency. Perhaps you hit 5 aces in your last match and made 60% of your first serves. You must disregard this if in most matches you rarely serve an ace and only succeed with 40% of your first serves. You also need to look at protecting your weaknesses from being exploited by your opponent's strengths.

Here is an example of a basic game plan and how it can be executed.

Your opponent: -

1: Likes to attack every second serve.

2: Hits the ball hard.

3: Sometimes becomes frustrated in long rallies.

4: Has a great forehand, but can miss under pressure.

5: Hits occasional powerful winners.

6: Prefers to hit passing shots down the line.

Now compare your game with your opponent's. You want to develop your plan where you utilise your strengths and minimise your weaknesses. Your strategy could be something like this:

Make more firsts serves so that they can't attack your second serve as much.

Use slower pace, hoping for errors from their forehand. They may hit some big winners but don't let that get to you. See if they can do it over and over again. They will probably begin to miss. Give 100% effort on each point, keeping your opponent on the court for as long as possible. Often serve to their forehand and take advantage when the return is short.

When you have devised your own game plan, focus on it completely. At the same time stay flexible as you may need to adjust it as the match proceeds. If you are against someone you have never played before, you must carry out this plan until you feel it needs changing, depending on how your opponent is playing.

Always change a losing game plan. Never change a winning one. In my experience, players sometimes give up their plans too early or leave things too late for it to make any difference. For example, you may decide to approach the net on mid court balls. You do this three times and each time get passed. Frustrated you give it up and try something else. This means you now have to rally from the baseline. Far better to have given the original plan more of a chance. Could your opponent have hit these passing shots on important points? You can't decide how someone really plays until you've seen them play the vital points in a match.

On the other hand, you could be using a losing game plan and not changing it in time. The score could be 6-1 6-0 5-2 in the third and you're still using the same method instead of adjusting it in the first set.

Also, when players give up their game plan they may be unsure what to do next and end up playing from point to point with no real structure. Players often panic at this stage and self doubt sets in. This affects their shot selection and performance.

If the game plan is failing what should you do? First, you need a plan 'b'. This helps you stay focused and maintains your confidence. Once again the plan needs to be within your own skills and capabilities.

Players can set a plan so outside their own ability that it is almost like an indirect way of quitting.

Changing a Game Plan

If you think a new plan would be more effective than an old one don't hesitate to change it. Make sure you have the skills to carry out your new strategy. There's no point deciding to serve and volley, for example, if net play is the weakest part of your game.

Matches are often won by successfully treading the margins between offensive and defensive play. The player who makes fewest errors usually wins the match. When you are considering changing a game plan the first thing to check is the number of errors you are making. The reason for being behind in the score will usually be found here. Perhaps you are pressing too much – going for the quick winner, rushing to get to the net or playing too many down the line shots when directing them across court would be safer and more the percentage option. The skill is to make fewer errors while not playing too defensively. On the other hand nerves at the start of a match may cause you to play too negatively and you could fall behind in the score. Again, recognise this and try to play more aggressively without resorting to chancy winners. These would inevitably only increase the number of errors. It is playing this fine line between offence and defence that is so often the secret of successful match play.

One way to cut out the number of errors is to ask someone to count them in a match. The errors will far out-number the winners. A quarter of these errors might be nothing more than basic rallying shots when all you intended perhaps was to hit the ball deep. Eradicating these kinds of mistakes, say from 45 to 30 in a 3 set match, could lift you into another class of player.

Another way to change the course of a match is to alter the tempo. You can do this within points or between them.

Slow balling is one method during the point. It means taking the pace off your shots, and hitting lots of high looping balls. Your opponent, who may have been leading and expecting a quick victory will now have to fight long and hard for success. The chances are they will become frustrated with your strategy, press for quick winners and in their turn start making errors. These will affect their confidence, especially if they were sailing through the match. Suddenly you will find the initiative is yours and that you have turned the whole tide of the match.

You can attempt something similar by changing the momentum between points. See how much time your opponent takes between points and games. Are they slow or do they prepare quickly? All you have to do is alter the tempo. Something as basic as that can affect their rhythm and concentration. Doubts set in, confidence fades as yours rises and the whole balance of the match is altered. One way of looking at a tennis match is the struggle to achieve and sustain a mental ascendancy over your opponent.

Stay committed with your new plan but flexible with your approach.

The following advice from international coach David Sammel offers advice on how to prepare for a 5 set match .

Build your Game - Mental Strength - Mental approach to a long match

Read and remember, or even take on court to read:

These tips were originally developed as a help for players about to play a Grand Slam or Davis Cup match for the first time. They had to mentally prepare for the possibility of going to five sets, which is a long time to concentrate.

When you may be on court for over three hours there is no point in trying to hype yourself up over a long period of time. If you get involved in a long match you need to pace yourself. However this does not mean low intensity, but rather keeping a good work ethic and choosing moments to raise your intensity.

I developed a tool to explain exactly what I mean by this and that is to imagine that your intensity is similar to that of a rev-counter in a car. The idea is to keep your rpms steady at a certain level of intensity. During important moments in the match you accelerate and raise the level with spurts of extra energy and intensity.

Imagine keeping the rpms at a constant 3000 rpms – then putting in spurts of intensity to 5000 rpms. Once the crisis passes you need to bring the revs back to 3000 rpms, so you do not burn out mentally or physically.

Below are the key points given to players which alleviate the fear of long matches. Although the information is aimed at preparing for five sets it is nevertheless valuable to all players who wish to learn how to manage their resources over a long match. It is also helpful if you are playing more than one match in a day.

Understand momentum will vary.

Try to stay sharp and finish in three sets if you can. You have plenty of time, but try to convert the early chance if it presents itself.

Keep your sense of humour and also your toughness. The crowd will feel this even if you are in a bad period.

Use your good tennis memories in times of crisis – Consciously prepare three successful memories to tap into for confidence.

Be you – the tennis player out there, feeling at home – rather than being manipulated by the crowds or your opponent. 'Own yourself' and therefore own your choice of emotions and actions.

Totally believe that you are competing to continue building your game and enjoy the reason for playing which is – performing your best under pressure.

When you serve or return for the match –look at your opponent, smile and play to take him/her out. Remember whatever you feel they are feeling worse because they are in the toughest position trying to stay alive in the match.

You can wake up the next morning with pride or regret. You will still be back learning and playing regardless. It is an honour but don't make it a bigger deal than any other tennis match played on a great court.

A player has four choices of what can happen when faced with a huge match with lots of pressure. He/she can choose either the route of worst or best outcome. Following are the most common reactions players will have to this kind of pressure:

Scene 1:

Nervous and scared: this means playing with frozen or lethargic legs, tentative, intimidated, overawed, can't think, believe it is a nightmare and be embarrassed.

Worst outcome - hardly remember the

match or remember it only as a blur, which will be no fun and a wasted opportunity.

Best outcome - snap out of it too late and realise how unnecessary it was to be that way. Tennis is what you do, not what is prearranged in the mind. There is huge regret for the wasted opportunity created by poor mental preparation.

Scene 2:

Nervous but adrenalized: can't time the ball and no breaks come your way.

Worst outcome – game racing away and then suddenly you become deflated and quiet. Match goes dead and you want it to end.

Best outcome – Understand adrenalin, so keep energised rather than manic and patient knowing that eventually you will get your eye in and will strike the ball well with nerves under control. Wait for your window, staying alive physically but calm mentally. Soon the match will be on!

Scene 3:

Nervous but energised: start like a dream taking the guy apart.

Worst outcome - opponent gets their window and starts to play well. You buy into the feeling that he/she is suddenly a better player, rather than realising it is a normal match with a change in momentum. You slide into panic and never recover your form.

Best outcome - realise it's a momentum change and keep physically working hard ut mentally calm therefore riding out the storm looking to taking your opportunities when they invariably arise.

Scene 4:

Start tough, keep tough and end tough –
enjoy it with a class performance.

"Empowering belief is the driving force behind your decisions, effort and focus."

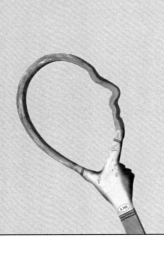

CHAPTER 7

Beliefs and Values

The Logical Levels Map is a valuable tool for organising your tennis, gathering information about your game and making the most of this information. The original model was developed by Robert Dilts and is based on the work of anthropologist Gregory Bateson and the philosopher Bertrand Russell.

Logical Tennis Levels

1. Vision
Where do you see yourself as a player?

2. Identity
Can you identify who are you are
as a person?

3. Beliefs, Values & Goals
What drives you? What are your values?

4. Capabilities & Skills
How are you going to do it?
Have you got the skills and talent?

5. Behaviour
What do you need?
Are you working hard on court?

6. Environment
When, where and with whom are you playing?
Are you competing?

In NLP this table is a most useful tool. It provides a structured way of understanding any system, in business, sport or everyday life. By using these Logical Levels we can recognise how the various levels interact with each other and how they are all related. It also helps you check relevant information, recognise problems and find solutions.

The bottom level on the table is the environment. This covers when and where you practice, with whom and on which type of surface.

The next level is behaviour: This looks at how you are on and off the court.

The third level is your capabilities and skills. This can include your technique, hand skills, co-ordination, footwork, racket control etc. Do you need to improve your tactics or your technical skills?

The next level is your beliefs, values and goals

Beliefs look at what you believe about yourself and your tennis. Some players may really believe they are the best but they lack the capabilities and skills. Another player may have all the shots but lacks self belief.

Empowering belief is the driving force behind your decisions, effort and focus. If I believe I can win a grand slam title, I will try harder, focus more intensely and do what ever it takes to achieve a desired outcome. Another example of an empowering belief is the fact that you are reading this book. I believed I could write it and turn it into a best selling tennis book. This belief drove me to focus, take action and produce the finished version. If I did not believe I could do it I would not have even started writing it. So these strong, empowering beliefs drive human behaviour and determine our decisions, goals and values.

Limiting Beliefs

Beliefs are extremely powerful and will influence every decision you make. Any negative ones will hold you back and stop you from taking action. They will affect how well you play in tough situations.

Some players really believe they are the best but don't have the skills or capabilities to get where they want to be. Other players may have the skills and capabilities but don't really believe in themselves. On the tennis logical levels table you will see all the areas that need to be in place and how one area relates to another.

For example, you might think, 'I don't believe I'm good enough to play matches.' Or 'In matches I "choke" and always lose.'

Write in any positive beliefs that you have such as: "I believe I can play in the first team" or "I am confident in my match play"

1. I am a good Doubles player

2. my Positioning around the Court is good

3. I am good at the net.

4. my fitness is getting better

5. my Backhand is strong

Write in any negative beliefs that are holding you back, such as "I believe I'm not good enough."

1. Lack Confidence { Don't think I'm good enough }

2. weak Serve { 1st e 2nd }

3. Frightened of letting partner down.

4. Put my self down

5. Crack under Pressure { give up }

Values

They may motivate you in a certain way. On the other hand perhaps you are unhappy with your tennis because one or more of your values is not being met. For example, if winning is your main priority and you have not won a match for the past six matches you would be unhappy with your game. In this case it would be helpful to focus on your performance rather than the outcome of your matches

There are two types of value – moving towards and moving away from them. Identify first what your core values are. What really matters to you in your tennis?

Think of a time when things were going really well and notice what comes to mind. Finding out what your values are will enable you to feel fulfilled with your tennis career. What were you doing at the time? Did you have any specific feelings that told you things were going well? Which core values were being fulfilled?

Now, recall a time when things were not going so well. What was the difference from the good time above? Which core values were not being fulfilled?

Here is a list of 8 common values.

Fun – exercise – winning – competing – playing my best – taking part – social aspects – learning new skills.

Write your own personal top 8 values in the space provided.

Moving Towards Values – You can guess what these are – Things you want to have in your life.

1.

2.

3.

4.

5.

6.

7.

8.

Now we need to find your moving away from values. These are feelings or experiences that you want to avoid - cheating – over competitive – looking bad – losing – playing poorly – getting angry – Over critical – not playing matches as well as in practice.

Write in your own.

1.

2.

3.

4.

5.

6.

7.

8.

You need to make sure your towards values are being fulfilled. If they are not, you must look at making some changes so that you meet more of your towards values and less of the away ones.

Honouring your values

The following questions will help you:

How are you expressing your values in your tennis at the moment?

Are any of your values not being met?

If yes, what needs to happen to change this?

How does your tennis fulfil or not fulfil your values?

When you look at these two areas, you may find certain beliefs are holding you back and stopping you from going for it.

We need to remember that all of our decisions are based around what we believe and what we value. Entering a certain tournament is based on what you believe i.e. Am I good enough to enter? And what you value i.e. If you value improving your performance you will no doubt enter. If on the other hand a value is moving away from losing then you may not want to enter a tournament where there is a chance you can lose.

Goals

These are the building blocks to desired ends or targets. They help us have a clear focus on what we want, driving us towards the target. In this book goals are also referred to as 'chunking' , breaking down large goals into manageable sizes. Goals also help us make progress and develop our games. Goals are an important way of helping players grow and reach their full potential. You should always record your progress so that when you look back over your goals you can see how much you have improved. In sports psychology goals are broken down into process, performance and outcome.

NLP goal-setting

(well formed outcomes, as outlined in chapter 4)

This process was developed by studying people who were good at setting and achieving goals, and who were happy with the results.

You may find it helpful to have another person talk you through the process. Explaining the details of your goals to them will uncover any parts that are vague, undefined, or problematic.

The second level on the table is your identity - the person you think you are. Can you see yourself as a world top 200 player? Can you identify with playing in your club's 1st team?

The top level is vision or mission. This looks at where you are heading and how you see the future. Perhaps you are in the third team and see yourself getting promoted to the second. You may want to take the lead in winning the division for your club. If you are a professional, your next target could be making the Wimbledon main draw or breaking into the top 100.

The great benefits of this table are that the levels are all inter-linked. If a positive change is made at one level a ripple effect runs through all of them. Take a player, for example, lacking self-belief. Improving their shots at the capabilities and skills level would help them gain self-belief as their confidence increases. This in turn impacts on the vision and identity level because they can now see themselves reaching the top league and feel it is a part of them.

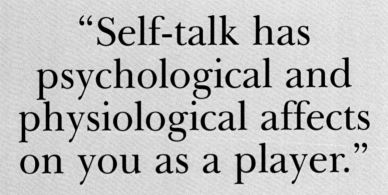

"Self-talk has psychological and physiological affects on you as a player."

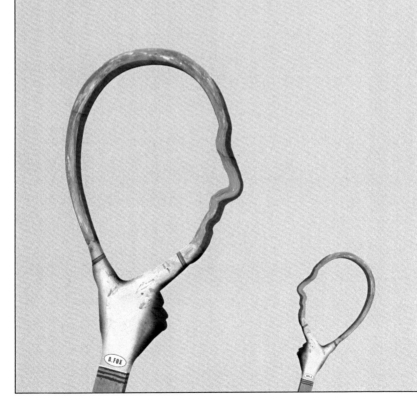

CHAPTER 8

Self Talk

Self-talk can make all the difference to your game. It is closely linked to your ability to focus. But treat it with care. You must understand how it affects your performance and the challenges you face.

There is positive self talk and negative.

Positive self-talk can improve self-esteem, motivation, focus (attention) and emotions. Tennis players often use specific words or cues to direct their focus on a given task. This keeps their mind on the task during a match rather than allowing it to wander.

Negative self-talk is destructive and self-demeaning. It lowers confidence, creates anxiety and loses concentration. The hardest thing about tennis is that once you start to beat yourself up it snowballs into a giant problem. You hear players calling themselves names or shouting at themselves after they lose a point or hit the ball into the net.

Self-talk also divides into the motivational and instructional.

Motivational self-talk helps players remain pumped up in a match and to stay calm in the heat of a battle. Players who are struggling in a match also use it. They might say, 'come on, you can fight back' or 'hang in there and break back' or 'I can do this'. There are no details about how to improve a shot or perform a specific skill.

Instead it is only used to keep you motivated during your match.

Instructional self-talk relates to improvement - 'place the ball more in front,' 'keep your wrist firm,' 'watch the ball.'

Self-talk in tennis normally has three different categories.

1: Cue words - 'breath control' or 'relax' or focus.'

2: Phrases - 'dig in' or 'attack forward' or 'stay tough.'

3: Sentences - 'keep focused in the present and forget the past' or 'reach up to the ball on my serve'.

Tennis players generally use phrases because they are short, to the point and get players focused and pumped up.

Self-talk does have psychological and physiological affects on you as a player. In NLP the words we use have an affect on the internal representations we make of the world. For example, you could be shouting at yourself for missing an easy backhand and hear a screaming voice inside your head yelling at you. This would in turn tighten up your body, make you feel under stress and lose your concentration. If you said the same words in a silly voice you might see the funny side. This, of course, would alter your 'state' and open up more resources for you to use in your match.

The point is that there is nothing good or bad but only the way you interpret the event. In reality, events are only events.

The way we construct or interpret them by the words we use, the mental images we build up and the physical state we put ourselves into, will all affect our views of the world and our reality. Imagine yourself shouting, using negative self-talk and beating yourself up after losing a match. Now compare this with the same words, but said in a funny cartoon voice. Which one made you laugh? Why did it make you laugh? Did you construct different images or representations? You should easily notice the difference.

You must also be aware that what you focus on will influence you. If you tell yourself how rubbish you are and that you can't play matches, this will soon show itself in your tennis. Focus on the positives. They will have a much more beneficial influence.

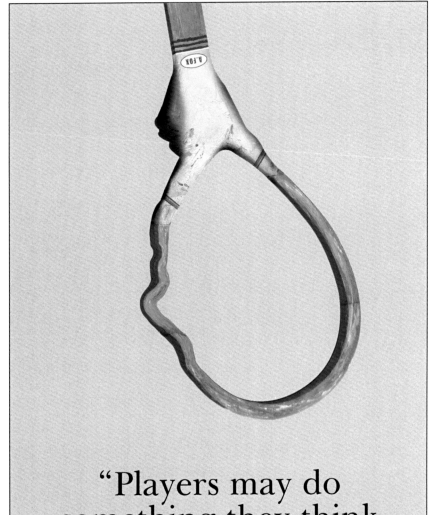

"Players may do something they think may bring them luck."

CHAPTER 9

Rituals and Routines

Routines are an important part of pre-match and post-match planning. They help keep you focused and prepare you to deal with events within and outside your control. Routines do several things. First, they help you to be organised so you can stay focused on the match. They also take away uncertain factors that can affect you. If you fail to prepare, you leave yourself open to uncontrollable events, such as the wind, sun, playing surface, bad calls, bad bounces and your opponent's behaviour.

Some players are superstitious. They may wear a cap they think brings them luck or perhaps they like to tie their laces in a certain way. This behaviour is linked to a good performance and has probably been reinforced in previous matches. In NLP this is called a complex equivalence. It means that when something happens it equals something else. For example: 'I'm playing on clay today so I will play my best tennis' or 'I have my lucky shirt on today so I will perform to my best'. This behaviour is similar to a placebo response where if you believe something will have a positive affect, then it probably will.

Pre-match routines should start the night before the match when sleeping and rest are needed. Of course, you must have the right amount of sleep. Eight hours is sufficient. Sleep can sometimes become a problem if you are unable to relax and switch off from thinking about the match.

Try to avoid alcohol the night before a match. It increases tiredness and can also cause you to wake up during the night. Try not to have caffeine before bedtime and avoid vigorous exercise late at night. The earlier you workout with a dynamic activity, the more deep you tend to sleep. Try and go to sleep at a regular time and include this as part of your routine. Avoid eating large meals late at night and cut down on any noise, cold or bright lights when sleeping.

A pre-match routine could look something like this:

Game Plan
Make 65% 1st serves, attack returns, and
take the ball early.

Rest
Have an early night.

Food and Drink
No alcohol or caffeine.
Drink water and eat pasta.

Checking Equipment
Check strings, towels, caps, grips and
anything else you have control over.
A copy of this book!

Stretch Routine
Do a gentle warm up, stretch main muscle
groups and loosen off.

Mental Preparation

Prepare mentally, using imagery
and positive self-talk. Stay alert
but not over excited.

Physical Warm-up

ave a practice session before the match.
Get warmed up, running through
each shot.

Blast Off

Step out onto court with confident
body language. Focus on timing the
shots and on your breath.

Good luck!

Bonus Sections

Non-verbal Communications:

The Psychological Importance of Body Language

Dr Andrew Peden

From the fist-pumping, point-winning celebrations of Lleyton Hewitt and Rafael Nadal - typically accompanied by the motivational imperatives to "Come on!" and "Vamos!" - to the slumped shoulders of Andy Murray following contested line calls and the frustrated racquet-smashing antics of Fernando Gonzalez after losing an important point, anyone who plays or watches tennis will be familiar with some of the ways in which players express their feelings on court through their behaviours. These are all extreme examples of what psychologists term 'non-verbal communications' or 'body language' – that is, any behaviour or communication that is not verbal or spoken aloud.

Non-verbal communications are not just powerful ways of expressing feelings and sending messages to people, they actually form the great majority of all our communications with others. Social psychologists have found that less than 10% of the messages we convey to others are in words; more that 90% of our communications are non-verbal, often through our tone of voice, the ways we make or avoid eye contact, our posture, hand gestures, movements and facial expressions, including subtle expressions of which most people are unaware, such as slight movements of the eyebrows.

Where there is a difference between

what a person says with their words and in their body language whilst they are speaking – that is, a mismatch between what they say and how they say it - we tend to place more emphasis on their non-spoken communication than on what they are saying. This is because people have less conscious control over their body language than their spoken language - meaning that if we can read our opponent's body language then we can read their true feelings, which can give us the edge in competitive tennis and be the difference between winning and losing.

Negative body language

Negative body language which signals nervousness includes clearing the throat, fidgeting, wringing of hands, hunched shoulders, massaging the temples, changes in the usual rate of breathing (typically breathing too fast) and quick, nervous head movements.

Negative body language which signals anger includes stiff posture, a tightened jaw, arms folded across the chest, intense eye contact, squared shoulders, tightened muscles, shallow breathing, clenched fists, holding the head in the palm of the hands, 'tutting' sounds, running your hand through your hair, rubbing the back of your neck, kicking at the ground or at an imaginary object.

During a tennis match you should avoid all of these negative body language signals, particularly slumped shoulders, dropping your head, looking to the sky in despair, vicious or angry swipes of your racquet after making a mistake or miss-hit, wildly hitting at balls between points in annoyance, making 'tutting' or similar sounds – because all of these non-verbal behaviours let your opponent know that he or she is getting under your skin. Knowing this will increase their motivation whilst your motivation is either in decline or so high that you are losing control. In his autobiography, Boris Becker made it clear that once he saw an opponent's shoulders slump, he knew that their resolve had been broken and at that point he would step-up his game in order to take advantage and win.

In many ways, negative body language is very similar to negative self-talk - that is, spoken language directed inwardly to the self, including thoughts, personal statements or words said aloud or privately inside one's head that are self-critical -

which simply leave you feeling bad about yourself and are counterproductive to winning tennis on all three psychological levels - the somatic (physical), the cognitive (thinking) and the behavioural (doing) – as they set up a vicious cycle of despair and hopelessness, leading ultimately to defeat. Being able to read your opponent's body language will give you a quick snapshot of how they are feeling and whether they are in control or losing confidence.

Positive body language

In sport as in life, it is important to show a positive mental attitude or 'PMA' – this will help increase effort, help maintain emotional stability and keep you calm on court - more focused, optimistic and energised and therefore more likely to improve your performance and win the game.

Firstly, in your non-verbal communications avoid all negative body language. Don't let your opponent see that you look defeated; don't let them know that fantastic winner you just hit was actually a mistake and went in a different area of the court from that which you aimed; don't let them know that the net court they just won a point on irritated or upset you.

Secondly, keep your body language positive at all times, even if it does not match with how you feel inside. Stand tall, hold your head high, don't grimace or scowl. Hold your head up and shoulders back and walk confidently. Positive body language includes a strong, firm handshake when meeting your opponent.

Lean forward, give them some eye contact and a smile. Show them that you are confident and secure in yourself and therefore in your ability.

Positive

Stand tall

Hold your head high

Pull your shoulders back

Walk confidently

Make eye-contact

Lean forward

Offer a firm handshake

Smile

Negative

Hunched or square shoulders

Shallow or rapid breathing

Clenched fists

Dropped head

Looking to the sky or kicking at the ground

Hitting at balls wildly

Tutting, sighing & clearing the throat

Massaging the temples

Holding head in hands

Rubbing back of neck

February 2007 adpeden@aol.com

Build in the mental part of your game.

by David Sammel.

Build your Game - Mental Strength – Psychological Warfare

The art of being able to rock your opponent and sow a seed of doubt is crucial to success in tennis.

I call this "finding a way to make a statement of intent". There are various ways of achieving this.

The eyes show focus and the intent to intimidate opponents

How to make a statement

Hit a 'Big Shot' from the baseline that is a winner.

Make a good play off opponent's best shot. (When you know what your opponent's favourite weapon is make a point of reading it once so you can reply with a tough shot)

Hit a service ace on a big point.

Hit three or four big first serves in a row.

Serve a bullet right at them. (This is also very effective as a second serve if your opponent continually stands in close and threatens your 2nd serve)

Stand in on 2nd serve. (Show you intend taking on your opponent's 2nd serve)

Show an opponent you are keen and

eager by making it plain you are going to attack their serve. You can do this with:

A good return.

Jigging and move about. Showing an opponent an aggressive look before the opponent serves.

Jogging to your chair if you have broken serve or have come close to breaking.

Dictate speed of the change of ends.

Bring opponent in and smack the passing shot straight at them.

Chip charge a second serve or hit and come in off a 2nd serve.

Bury a smash.

Hit a big shot off a powerful 1st serve. Read one so you can anticipate it early achieving a solid hit.

By changing your return position, give your opponent a totally different look before they serve. (It must be obvious enough for him/her to notice. You can do this by standing closer in, further back or over to one side.)

Make noise as you hit the ball. (Louder grunt or exhalation of air.)

Use humour. (After they've hit a winner you could smile and acknowledge their shot. When you've missed a sitter smile and turn away. If they hit a ball straight at you just give a wry smile)

Stand tall with a solid stare down the court before you serve.

Give a lingering look of satisfaction after a good volley. Show speed and determination to chase every ball with the intent to hit them back with control.

Strong raised fist after a break of serve.

The aggressive self talk "I can do this! I love fighting for every point! I can fight and be cool in my mind at the same time!"

The aggression to use the first chance you get after they have made a statement. (This is a huge key to recovering your composure when you have been hurt by your opponent's big play)

First point of a game. Hit a big serve, or serve and volley to show you intend winning the game strongly. On return, try to attack or return a solid ball with full focus again, to show that your opponent will have to fight for every point to hold serve.

If you are totally out of the match be prepared to do something entirely different to swing the momentum your way. (Sudden drop-shot, a game with no pace, going for high-risk winners for a game, or even a 1st serve underarm).

Mental Preparation

by Dave Sammel

The Serve and Volleyer

The serve and volleyer expects many free points and wants the opponent to develop a complex about their return of serve. He thinks that if he can volley away some good returns and passing shots early in the match, the opponent will panic and start to try for better and better returns and passes. When a serve and volleyer serves well it is easy to feel that they are unbreakable.

How to Counter

Try to make as many returns off the first serve as you can, even if it gives him an easy volley. Giving the serve volleyer a high volume of balls to put away pays off later in the match when the pressure is high.

Attack the second serve, not specifically with pace, but by moving up the court to get the ball back faster and rush the volleyer. It is then very important to make him volley for a second time or hit an overhead. Do not go for rash passes off good volleys – make him play. Again, the pay-off comes later in the match!

Be patient – Do not panic but sit and wait for the loss of focus – the game that has a double fault, the missed volley or several service faults. It often happens after one or two great service games.

Try to hit as many returns to the feet as possible, not neglecting the return down the middle.

1. The Good Returner

This player makes a high number of returns and hits the ball well in front, rushing the server. He wants to create the following feelings: -

Server getting nervous not knowing where to serve to get an easy point

Σ Server is afraid of the return and therefore does not serve and volley anymore

How to Counter

Serve into the body more. It is harder to step into the ball when it is coming at you. Do not look for the easy point and expect a return. Do not rush the first shot or volley – make him play his second shot of the rally. They rely on quick points. This player is a tough customer so do not panic.

Run hard and work hard to give him a high volume of second shots.

Σ Keep your 1st serve percentage high by mixing in a lot of _ speed serves. Also use a mixture of spins to prevent the class returner from settling into a routine, knowing what to expect.

Σ Try to mess up his range by mixing up the serve and volley game. In other words, sometimes wait for the return, then go in and take a few more chances with bigger second serves.

Σ Don't give him easy games on his own service. This allows him to concentrate exclusively on his strong point – breaking you with good returns.

2. The Clay Court Specialist

This player will wear you down until you lose reason and patience and start slashing at balls looking for a quick winner, or attacking the net without rushing and unbalancing him first.

How to Counter:

If you are not a similar player you know you have to attack well – therefore most important is your frame of mind. Accept that:

a)   You will be passed

b)   You will watch some top spin lobs land

c)   It may take you a while to break him down

d)   You need to look forward to the

moment when he actually becomes erratic and gives you a few freebies

Method of Attack:

a) Your own serve is your biggest weapon in this fight – use it well to keep them off balance. Approximately 60% three-quarter pace first serves, concentrating on placement (including to the body) so that your first serve percentage remains high. 40% hard serves so he can never settle down to one pace and you get a few free points.

b) Serve and volley some of the time especially at 30-40, 40-30 and advantage points

c) The two big shots in your attack arsenal after the serve are the second shot off the return and the return of serve. If the second shot is a volley, volley behind the player a lot and cut off volleys short (not drop volleys but turning away volleys cross court)

d) When the second shot is off a shorter return you must attack the ball to take command of the point and create chances for the "cut in".

e) When you attack the net do not forget one of the most neglected approach shots – deep down the middle to jam them up and take away a clay-courter's lifeblood – passes made on the run creating angles. Play the down the middle shot to force him to hit a backhand e.g. if he regularly runs round the backhand (to hit inside-out forehands) then your "down the middle shot" might actually be further over to his backhand side.

Return of Serve

a) Make a high volume of returns off first serves using height. Do not be too proud to stand well back to achieve this. As you get used to his serve, you can step up into the court to rush him more.

b) Returning second serve – step up into the court, hit it early and attack it to rush him and take control of the point. (Remember hitting a ball early and attacking it does not mean rushing or hitting hard only.) If you see the opponent is in trouble, cut in and volley and sometimes approach directly after the return.

Warning

Just because you hit a good second shot or return does not mean that you keep control of the point. Often the opponent will counter with good length and spin. In this case, settle down and play the point looking for an opportunity to attack. Do not press to take control – play for it

3. The Net Rusher

A net rusher wants to rush until you panic. The player often approaches the net on a "bluff" and relies on the pressure of you having to pass him so often that it wears you down.

How to Counter

Σ Watch the ball and play your shots as you normally would, ignoring the odd, amazing dive volley! Once he knows you are not rushed to pass him and do not mind him winning a fair share of the points when he has hit a good approach shot, this player has little left.

Σ Make the opponent play a lot of volleys and overheads.

Σ Take any chance you get to go in. Rarely do "chip and charge merchants" hit good passing shots themselves

4. Big Hitter

This player tries to blast you off the court and overpower you. He will usually start well and is a good front runner. Awesome when playing well, however:

How to Counter

Hustle and use height. It is imperative that this player is made to hit big shots to win the point as often as possible.

Σ Swing early and meet his big shots in front so you can use his pace to get in on him. Making him hit passing shots forces the pace, causing him to hit hard and lose control. Your state of mind - ignore his great shots, work hard and do not be intimidated; be convinced he will run out of big shots if he has to hit enough of them. Once he begins to miss and hesitate, it's over.

5. *The Deceptive Player*

This player wants to break your rhythm and more importantly prevent you from establishing any rhythm at all. He will mix up and rush you by deceptive play because he holds the ball on the strings well. He mixes pace, and varies his serves, can generate surprising pace when moving forward on the ball, and times a return off a big serve. A very difficult customer, however.

How to Counter

Σ Apart from possibly the serve they have few gears to step up the pace

Σ Their game is based on timing. With fewer margins for error they move the ball around to create angles. They are prone to making mistakes in batches.

Σ Play back to the opponent, e.g. if he hits a cross-court angle, hit the ball back cross-court in order to reduce the angles, unless you feel confident of hitting a winning shot down the line.

Σ Get under the ball well to keep a good length because then it is harder for them to move the ball around. It also leads to important approach opportunities. Be low, alert and agile at the net because if you start to read the passes from this player, he is dead because he cannot beat you with pace. Stay low, to give them a problem – the heavy ball!

Σ Your state of mind – do not be concerned if you feel disjointed or unbalanced by this player at times – you cannot avoid it. He will mess you about with little cuts and you need to thrust a sword through him before you bleed to death. Get him to feel over-powered by hitting big shots, volleys, serves and overheads when you get a chance. Don't get cute and try to out manoeuvre him when you can kill the ball

Σ If you play the same way as this player – play the percentages more

Within the above styles of player, you may also need to take into account the following characteristics:

6. The Cut In Specialist

Don't watch for him coming in. Watch the ball and realise that when in trouble sometimes go for the big shot. Off the backhand slice, go down the line because this is the most difficult place from which to hit an effective volley

7. The All Rounder

Play your game and wait because even these solid players make mistakes. You must take some chances to unbalance them.

8. Very Tall Players and Very Quick Players

Hit directly at tall players when they are at the net. The lob is not wasted because if they hang back sometimes it is easier to get the ball at their feet.

Very quick players recover quickly and can reach shots that are played away from them relatively easily. Therefore, a good tactic is often to place the ball behind them in the spot they have just come from, thus wrong footing the player.

An example of good mental preparation
for a performance player in tournaments.

1. Before you play a match prepare twice. Once, the night before, seeing yourself as you want to be in the match. Picture good balance, flowing strokes and trusting yourself in key situations. Then have a brief preparation before you play – a quick recap when you deal with any anxiety you might be feeling before you step out onto the court.

2. Take a note onto the court with some key points/phrases to read to help

recapture focus if you lose concentration. Write any key phrases that work for you.

3. Keep building the same house – each match and each practice. Win or lose try to keep learning – and have a structured course you are following so you build consistently rather than jumping from one quick fix to another.

4. Don't get caught up in success or expectations. Tennis is something you do i.e. play shots, get lower, watch better etc. Can you do winning, or expectations or success? These are only the outcome of good doing, so focus on the doing.

5. Enjoy it all – on and off court – but keep an edge to your focus. Remember that you may have a long and successful tennis career ahead – this means playing many tournaments so no single event will make

or break your career.

6. All the above takes for granted a key ingredient which is most important of all. A player must have an intense desire to compete and fight for the win every time he/she steps out onto the match court. Combine this attitude with the perspectives and intelligence stated in the above points and any player is a powerful opponent.

FAQs from young players and parents

How do we decide which are the best tournaments to play and how do we build a schedule?

The first step is to sit down with an annual Planner and put in the most important tournaments, which are listed below:

1. The National Championships for your age group and the qualifying events for this tournament if you are not rated high enough for direct entry.

2. In the UK the next most important are the Winter Grand Prix events and the summer clay court tournaments. Each country will have its own unique hierarchy of events that your Federation or Tennis association can tell you about if you are beginning your tennis tournament journey.

3. Your priorities will depend on your age and standard and will determine which tournaments to enter. A good general rule to follow until you are out of juniors is to regard playing in National Championships as essential. This in my view allows you to evaluate where you are in relation to your

peers and how competitive you are nationally. It also gives the national coaches a chance to see you and how you compete.

Σ Another crucial aspect of the schedule is to put in an annual holiday of two weeks and possibly another break of a week when you leave your rackets behind or at the very least only indulge in some social tennis and not feel it is part of a structured routine. If other children in the family are not involved in tennis taking a break like this has a positive effect on the whole family. The time spent travelling to weekend tournaments and school holiday events can affect the whole family and makes it seem to revolve around the tennis player.

The basic structure for planning the route forward is to know where you are in terms of your rating or ranking so you can plan at the correct level. This changes as you progress.

Here are the different level of tournaments for the UK leading to international events with an indication as to why you should play them. Other countries will have similar tournaments and again you can find this out from your local associations or Coaches associations. Your individual coach should also be able to advise you. If your coach cannot advise you perhaps you ought to question his or her commitment or knowledge.

Mini tennis and local club events

Level: Beginners and players starting out on the adventure of tennis competition.

There are different levels of mini tennis identified by colour. See the LTA website for participating clubs which will help parents decide where to start their children.

County/Regional Matchplays

Level: Tournament starters, which will allow you to gain a national rating if you are over 10 years of age. There are numerous age group events ranging from U10's, 11's, 12's etc to U16

National rating tournaments run by clubs

Level: Rated players competing regularly and beginning to think about taking competitive tennis to a level where they can enter the National Championship qualifiers. There is a tournament book, which lists all these tournaments by region, age groups and ratings bands. Again your national governing body will be able to advise on this and also send you tournament schedules.

National Junior Events

Level: A regular competitor who is competing nationally and committed to travelling long distances to compete. This player is beginning to understand the pathway to national success. These tournaments include regional challenge events, Grand Prix's and spring clay court events all of which have been outlined in point 3 above.

European Tennis Association (ETA) Tournaments with a view to a European age group ranking

Level: A regular competitor who is

competing nationally and committed to traveling long distances to compete. This player is beginning to understand the pathway to international tennis success and is already experiencing home success at national level. There are under(U)12, U14 and U16 events all over Europe and the schedule and rules can be found on the website www.eta.com.

International Tennis Federation (ITF)
under 18 world ranking tournaments

Level: Direct acceptances into the main draw into the nationals. These players are seriously considering eventually playing full time tennis and are becoming top performers at home. Girls will begin with these at 13-15 years of age and boys at 14-16

Players begin with group 5 tournaments

and as they attain and build higher world rankings they move up the ladder into group 4, 3, 2 and finally group 1 events. Group A events are the junior Grand Slam tournaments played the second week of the Australian, Wimbledon, French and US Opens. wwwitfjuniors.com

Senior Money Tournaments and National Circuits

Level: Good national standard juniors and aspiring pros or good senior players. Established pros sometimes play for match practice and when returning from injury. Most countries have a circuit or a number of club tournaments at senior level that pay prize money. These count towards national rankings but do not carry any international ranking points.

ITF futures and satellite tournaments

Level: Players beginning the pro tour and players trying to improve their world rankings. The men are chasing an ATP (Association of Tennis Professionals) ranking and the women a WTA (Women's Tennis Association) ranking. The level of player competing at this level range from unranked to about 300 in the world. These are worldwide and organized by the ITF although the European tournaments for women are organized by the ETA.

The final levels of tournaments are Challengers (players generally ranked between 125 and 400) and the main tours. At this stage of your career you will not need the advice of any website when it comes to planning your tournament programme.

Stay in the present
Jim Edgar

Jim Edgar has been one of Britain's most successful teaching professionals over the last 20 years. A late starter to the sport, Jim was 14 years old when he began playing at Hale Tennis Club in South Manchester, eventually becoming a 5 time senior County Champion for Cheshire. Jim took up full time coaching after graduating from University in 1986. Jim has coached at all levels and has worked with many top ranked British players including Justin Layne, Simon Dickson, Daniel Kiernan, Jonathan Marray and David Sherwood.

For the past 5 years some of Jim's pupils have been represented at Wimbledon. Jonathan Marray and David Sherwood in the Men's doubles event in 2002 and 2003. At the 2005 Championships 17 year old Chris Llewellyn reached the semi final of the Junior Doubles event partnered by Juergens Strydom of Namibia.

Jim was a speaker at the 2006 British Tennis Coaches Annual conference and is currently based at the Bolton Arena.

'Learn to focus on what really matters during your matches.'

Sports psychologists will tell you that you need to have an IPS (Ideal performance state) during matches. Steve Renwick has covered this subject in this excellent book and by now you are well on the way to becoming a mentally astute match player.

When it comes to the crunch in matches, however, it is easy to fall back into bad old habits. The set points, break points, and match points that we have to deal with can still destroy our clear focus and send us back into a state of panic. If this still happens to you, consider whether your attitude to match play could be altered in your favour.

The table below gives you a choice of 3 ways of looking at how you deal with stress when the pressure is really on in matches, especially after you have just made an unforced error on an important point: -

Do you remind yourself of all the times this has happened in the past and believe that you will always repeat this behaviour?

Do you constantly look ahead to the future wishing the match was over and you have won?

Or

Do you enjoy the immediate challenge of playing each point and focus only on what you are doing in the present?

Past

"I THINK ABOUT WHAT HAS HAPPENED."

this brings

GUILT AND FRUSTRATION

I think about all the mistakes I have made in the past.

I can't think clearly about my game plan because I focus on my previous errors and this erodes my confidence further.

Every match I lose makes me more doubtful about achieving the success I crave.

I get really nervous on the big points because I remind myself of all the times I have blown it in the past.

I am always too nervous to play my best tennis in matches. I am much better in practice.

Present

"I THINK ABOUT WHAT I AM GOING TO DO."

POSITIVE CHALLENGE

I take each point one at a time. I am clear about the game plan I must carry out and have the strength to do it.

The most important thing in the match is sticking to my strategy and not doubting my ability to carry it out.

*I play points one at a time with 100%
commitment. After each point I prepare for
the next point having forgotten about what
happened in the last point.*

*I have patience and composure in my tennis.
I am relaxed about the result. I focus on my
performance not the result of the match.*

*I love the challenge of matches. If I compete
well I am happy whatever the result.*

Future

"I THINK ABOUT WHAT MIGHT HAPPEN."

this brings

ANXIETY AND PRESSURE

I am worried and anxious about whether I can win this match.

The result is all that I am interested in.
I do not care how I achieve the win.
I am desperate for quick success.

Every mistake makes me more scared that I may lose. My confidence is totally dependent on the score.

I get really nervous on the big points because the result is so important to me.

I tend to overplay in matches. I try too hard to win and usually end up beating myself with unforced errors.

It is often said that the definition of insanity is continuing to do the same thing but expecting a different outcome. If you play your tennis matches in the past or the future and expect your results to improve, then you're crazy! They won't. You will just keep getting more of the same and ultimately you will not enjoy the thrill of competition.

Did you see anything in the table above that describes your match play behaviour? If you are not yet in the central column you must act now to stop being a better practice player than match player.

The most important thing to focus on is your game plan. How are you trying to play? What tactics are you using? Your tennis coach should have helped you develop a clear strategy for playing taking advantage of your strengths and covering up your weaknesses. This is your method of play (or game plan) that you will use in your matches. Of course it needs to be flexible to deal with different opponents but you will not usually deviate greatly from it. For example if you are a serve and volleyer that is what you must do. There is little point in staying on the baseline and grinding out 50 shot rallies if your ground strokes are unreliable! Do what you do best and have the conviction to see it through to the end taking each point at a time. By focusing on your game plan you also depersonalise the match process. It is your game plan against your opponents, not really you against him/her. If you didn't win the match you can evaluate the match in terms of how well your game plan worked rather than blaming yourself. All top players focus on this process rather than the outcome when they evaluate their matches and of course every player can improve their game plan.

Staying in the present means exactly

that, being totally focussed at this moment. What does this really mean? What am I supposed to be focussed on?

The BALL of course!! Watch the ball really intently when you are under pressure. Try to see its seams clearly, look to see the manufacturers logo and try to watch ball until it is on your strings. Most mistakes at all levels of tennis are due to not properly watching the ball. If you practice focusing on the ball in practice you will feel more relaxed and appear to have more time to play your shots. Practice this until it becomes second nature and when you start playing matches you are much more likely to keep your focus on the ball.

Finally, remember that playing a sport as difficult as tennis at a competitive level will stretch you physically and mentally into some uncomfortable places. You must embrace the thrill of competition and not burden yourself by concentrating on the result. Accept that you may lose and that you may also win. It is the uncertainty at the beginning of the match that is the best part of tennis. If you switch on your TV to watch Federer against Nadal in the French Open final and you already know who will win, it won't be very exciting! The exciting part is how the match flows, the changes in momentum and the unexpected twists in fortune. The greatest matches all develop like this and so will your matches. Accept that if you perform well and stay in the present you should be proud of yourself whatever the outcome.

To sum up; focus on your performance and not the result; watch the ball on each shot and stay in the present; enjoy the thrill of competition rather than be scared of it.

Good luck!

jimedgar@boltonarena.com

www.jimedgar.co.uk.